1   Introduction

Punitive damages can improve economic efficiency in cases where an injurer has a chance of escaping liability. Under these circumstances, compensatory damages alone are not sufficient for optimal deterrence since the injurer will not internalize the full cost of the harm. The standard law and economics approach is to base the punitive damages on the injurer's probability of escaping liability. However, several scholars[1] argue that this approach may lead to excessive awards if the payment of punitive damages to one victim increases the other victims' probability of collecting damages. In other words, successful verdicts can create information (i.e., publicity) for others. For example, media coverage of a large punitive award against a cigarette manufacturer might induce other smokers to sue that same manufacturer.

This paper derives the optimal punitive award when there is a possibility that publicity increases the other victims' probability of collecting damages. As compared to the standard approach where the probability remains unchanged, the result is a lower optimal punitive award. The difference between these two awards increases in the (i) likelihood of publicity, (ii) strength of publicity, and (iii) number of victims.

The introduction of these three parameters into the calculation of the optimal punitive award certainly increases the information burden on efficiency-minded judges. However, the payoff is a more accurate award that does not excessively deter productive activities. It is likely that this information burden will be lower for appellate court judges than for lower court judges. Presumably, by the time of an appeal, judges will be able to directly observe, rather than estimate, one or more of these parameters. At the very least,

---

[1] See Polinsky and Shavell (1998), Viscusi (1998), and Cooter and Ulen (2000).

1

the analysis provides a framework for judges to incorporate publicity when determining punitive awards.

In addition to modifying the optimal punitive multiplier, the paper explores the efficiency effects of awarding different punitive amounts depending on *when* a victim initiates a suit relative to the other victims. The result is that, under certain litigation cost conditions, moving from uniform to different punitive awards is an improvement in efficiency. The logic is that, unless the first victims receive a premium, they might not have the incentive to litigate, which prevents a possible positive externality (i.e., publicity).

Section 2 reviews the economic research that addresses publicity and punitive damages. Section 3 develops the publicity model and examines the efficiency of heterogeneous punitive awards. Using the framework developed in the model, Section 4 analyzes *BMW of North America, Inc. v. Gore*, a recent U.S. Supreme Court case that involved a large punitive damage award. Section 5 concludes the paper. All proofs, except for Proposition 5, are in Appendix A.

2   Background

Becker (1968), focusing on criminal acts and escaping liability, is one of the earliest works to conclude that the magnitude of the punishment should be inversely related to the probability of punishment. Cooter (1982, 1989), Landes and Posner (1987), and Shavell (1987, p. 161) apply the "inverse-rule" to tort law and product liability. However, a number of studies, under a variety of scenarios, have re-examined the ability of the inverse-rule, or standard approach, to reach optimal deterrence.

Under circumstances where risk-averse victims are also customers of the injurer, Craswell (1996) finds the optimal punitive award could be higher or lower than under the standard approach. The ambiguity stems from the fact that higher punitive awards result in higher prices. If victims successfully collect damage payments in court, then they are compensated for the price increase. However, the unsuccessful victims are simply left with higher prices. They would prefer lower punitive damages and lower prices, which reduces the variance of income. For corporate environmental and safety torts, Viscusi (1998) finds no empirical support for the deterrence effect of punitive awards. Therefore, if we take into account the practical difficulty of assessing the punitive award, Viscusi suggests an optimal punitive award of zero for these torts.

Although the above studies indicate that the inverse-rule is not applicable in all situations, it remains the benchmark measure for calculating the optimal damage award. Even if we accept the applicability of the standard approach, a number of studies have commented on the key parameter: the probability of collecting damages. Polinsky and Shavell (1998, p. 895) highlight the possibility that the amount of the damage payment and the probability of collecting damages are endogenous. If so, a higher punitive award results in a higher probability of litigation, which lowers the optimal punitive award. In turn, this lower award decreases the probability of litigation, which increases the optimal punitive award. Viscusi (1998, p. 313) also alludes to this idea when he contends that juries who do not take a dynamic view of punitive damages might award excessively high amounts, which would cause more settlements and create an overall snowball effect on payments. Cooter and Ulen (2000, p. 353) also mention that awarding punitive damages will likely increase the *ex ante* probability of liability. All three observations assume a definitive relationship between awarding punitive damages and the probability of collecting damages.

This paper develops a more flexible approach to modeling the information value of punitive damage awards to future litigants. This flexibility is desirable because awarding punitive damages will increase the other victims' probability of collecting damages *only if* they know about it. Otherwise, the original probability of collecting damages is the correct number to use in the punitive award calculation. However, if a court awards punitive damages *and* it is publicized, then Polinsky and Shavell, Viscusi, and Cooter and Ulen's point becomes valid. The following section expands on these thoughts into a formal publicity model of punitive damages.

3   Model

3.1   Setup

Assume that the injurer is a firm that causes a level of harm, H, to each of the n victims. Thus, the total amount of social harm is equal to their product: nH. The harm could be in the form of insurance fraud targeted at the elderly, a faulty medical device that gives imprecise readings, a flawed tire design, and so forth. The following figure summarizes, for each victim, the possible events that could occur subsequent to the harm.

Figure 1:   **Harm**

$$(1-p_1) \qquad\qquad p_1$$
$$[no\ detection] \qquad [detection]$$

$$(1-\ell) \qquad\qquad \ell$$
$$[no\ liability] \qquad [liability]$$

$$(1-z) \qquad\qquad z$$
$$[no\ change \qquad\quad [change$$
$$in\ p_1] \qquad\qquad in\ p_1\ to\ p_2]$$

Thus, for a particular victim, there is a positive probability that the firm's harm will not be detected, $(1-p_1)$. We can think of "detection" in two ways, depending on the context. First, we can assume that the victims do not know they are harmed, and detection occurs when a victim finds out about the harm.[2] Alternatively, we can assume that all victims know they are harmed, and detection occurs when a victim determines who is responsible.

If the harm *is* detected, then there is a possibility that the firm will not be held liable, $(1-\ell)$.[3] Otherwise, the firm is held liable and pays a damage payment equal to D. The damage payment is defined as the sum of the compensatory, C, and punitive, X, damages:

$$D = C + X, \tag{3.1.1}$$

where the compensatory damages are assumed to equal the harm done:

---

[2] This is more likely for financial harms such as fraud but can also apply to physical harms such as carcinogens.

[3] This second probability of escaping liability can be dropped without a loss of generality. Essentially, it introduces the possibility that an injuring firm escapes liability even though the harm was actually done. For certain harmful acts, such as criminal health care fraud, the probability of escaping liability is likely to be low given that, in fiscal year 1997, 76.95% of the fraud cases prosecuted resulted in a conviction (U.S. Department of Justice (1997)).

$$C = H. \tag{3.1.2}$$

Furthermore, if the victim is successful in collecting damages, then there is a chance that the verdict will be publicized. For example, a local farmer who successfully sues an insecticide manufacturer for cancer might alert other farmers who use the same fertilizer of their exposure to a carcinogen. This publicity would result in a revision in the probability of detection for the subsequent victims. If the revision does not occur after the first successful verdict, it could occur after the second, and so forth; however, once the revision occurs, there are no other subsequent revisions. In sum, there is positive probability, z, that the original probability of detection, p_1, changes to p_2 where $p_2 > p_1$.[4] It is assumed that there are no subsequent revisions after p_1 changes to p_2.[5] (Alternatively, z could represent the chance that future litigation will be more successful, i.e., $\ell_1 < \ell_2$, given the punitive award.) Theoretically, the probability of detection might never change from the original p_1 for all of the victims; however, with more victims, it is less likely that the probability remains at p_1.[6] Given this framework, the following sections will derive the optimal damage payment, including punitive damages, under a range of assumptions.

3.2   Expected Damages

---

[4] This assumption is supported by a finding in Garber and Bower (1999) where, from 1983 to 1996, they find almost no newspaper articles reporting on the 259 automotive product liability verdicts in favor of the defendants. Thus, publicity is likely to occur only after the plaintiffs are successful, which will increase the probability of detection.

[5] Conceivably, the probability of detection could change after each successful verdict. Assuming the first revision is typically the most important, I believe the benefit of this simplification (i.e., model tractability) outweighs the cost (i.e., generalization).

[6] Moreover, the probability of detection might only change for some victims. However, this model assumes publicity affects all victims' behavior uniformly.

When making its decision regarding the harmful product or practice, the firm will consider both the *expected* benefits and costs. Included in the expected cost calculation is what the firm expects to pay the victims of the harm. If we let i represent a victim where $i \in 1,...,n$, then the expected damage payment to the statistical first victim ($i = 1$) is

$$E(D_1) = (1 - p_1)0 + p_1[(1 - \ell)0 + \ell D_1],$$ (3.2.1)

which reduces to

$$E(D_1) = p_1 \ell D_1.$$ (3.2.2)

Therefore, the product of the probability of detection, p_1, and liability, ℓ, is the probability that the injurer actually pays the damage payment, D. Thus, *ex ante*, the injuring firm makes its decision based on the statistical payment of $p_1 \ell D_1$.

If we generalize to all the victims, then the probability of publicity, z, becomes relevant. Thus, the expected damage payment to victim i is

$$E(D_i) = (1 - \theta)^{i-1}[p_1 \ell D_i] + (1 - (1 - \theta)^{i-1})[p_2 \ell D_i],$$ (3.2.3)

where $\theta = p_1 \ell z$, which represents the probability that the publicity actually changes the other victims' probability of detection. The logic behind θ is that a certain victim must (1) detect the harm, p_1, (2) win the lawsuit, ℓ, and (3) have publicity, z, before the probability of detection is revised. Thus, the probability that the ith victim detects with probability p_1 is $(1 - \theta)^{i-1}$, while $1 - (1 - \theta)^{i-1}$ represents the probability the victim detects with probability p_2. Note that when $i = 1$, equation (3.2.3) simplifies to (3.2.2). However, as i gets larger, the likelihood that the ith victim will detect with probability p_1 diminishes since $(1 - \theta)^{i-1}$ gets smaller.

It follows that the total expected damage payment, $E(TD)$, for the harmful

activity is the sum of (3.2.3) for all the n victims:

$$E(TD) = \sum_{i=1}^{n} E(D_i) = \sum_{i=1}^{n} (1-\theta)^{i-1} A + (1-(1-\theta)^{i-1})B, \qquad (3.2.4)$$

where $A = p_1 \ell D_i$ and $B = p_2 \ell D_i$. Optimal deterrence is achieved when the injurer

makes *ex ante* decisions that internalize the full social cost of the harm imposed on the

victims, nH. In other words, efficiency is realized when

$$E(TD) = nH. \qquad (3.2.5)$$

3.3   Punitive Damage Multiplier

First, let us assume that there is no chance that a successful verdict will be

publicized ($z = 0$); thus, it follows that the probability of detection never deviates from

the original p_1. Additionally, assume that there are no punitive awards ($X = 0$).

From equation (3.2.3), if the victims are guaranteed to collect damages

($p_1 = \ell = 1$), with only compensatory damages, the expected damage payment to victim i

reduces to

$$E(D_i) = H. \qquad (3.3.1)$$

The reason is that if $\theta = 0$, $p_1 = \ell = 1$, and $D_i = H$, then $E(D_i) = p_1 \ell D_i = H$ with no

punitive damages. Thus, the expected total damage payment for all the n victims is

$$\sum E(D_i) = nH. \qquad (3.3.2)$$

Since the injuring firm expects to pay the full social cost of the harm, efficiency is

achieved.

If $0 < p_1 < 1$ and $0 < \ell \leq 1$, then the injuring firm has some chance of escaping the damage payment. If we hold the assumption that only compensatory damages are awarded ($X = 0$), and there is still no chance of publicity, then the expected damage payment to victim i is

$$E(D_i) = p_1 \ell H, \tag{3.3.3}$$

and the total expected damage payment is

$$\sum E(D_i) = p_1 \ell n H, \tag{3.3.4}$$

which is less than the efficient level, nH, since $p_1 < 1$. Thus, when there is a positive probability of escaping payment and no punitive damages, the firm will not internalize the full cost of the social harm.

With punitive damages ($X > 0$), the level of damage payment, D_i^*, that solves the following equation:

$$\sum E(D_i) = \sum_{i=1}^{n} p_1 \ell D_i = nH, \tag{3.3.5}$$

which must hold for optimal deterrence, is

$$D_i^* = \frac{H}{p_1 \ell}. \tag{3.3.6}$$

Recalling that $D = C + X$, the punitive part of the damage award can be represented as

$$X_i^* = D_i^* - C = \frac{H}{p_1 \ell} - H = \frac{1 - p_1 \ell}{p_1 \ell} H, \tag{3.3.7}$$

and D_i^* can be rewritten as

$$D_i^* = H + \frac{1 - p_1 \ell}{p_1 \ell} H, \tag{3.3.8}$$

where $\dfrac{1-p_1\ell}{p_1\ell}$ is the punitive multiplier. Assuming risk-neutrality, equation (3.3.7) is the standard result when analyzing how high to set the punitive award. It follows that the higher the likelihood of escaping liability, $1-p_1\ell$, the higher the optimal punitive multiplier.

3.4 Extension

If we assume that publicity is possible ($0 < z < 1$) and there are no punitive awards ($X = 0$), then there is a possibility that the probability of detection, p_1, changes after a verdict. Again, let $0 < p_1 < 1$ and $0 < \ell \le 1$. Since $D_i = H$, it follows that the injurer's total expected damage payment is

$$\sum E(D_i) = \sum_{i=1}^{n}(1-\theta)^{i-1}A' + (1-(1-\theta)^{i-1})B', \qquad (3.4.1)$$

where $A' = p_1\ell H$ and $B' = p_2\ell H$. Equation (3.4.1) is less than the efficient level, nH, since $p_1 < 1$, which implies $A' < H$. When $A' < H$, there is insufficient deterrence since the injurer expects to pay the first victim A', which is less than the actual harm done, H.

With punitive awards ($X > 0$), then there are two approaches to optimality. First, one could achieve optimal deterrence with different punitive awards. Following equation (3.3.6), the optimal damage award would be:

$$D_i^* = \frac{H}{p_i\ell} \qquad (3.4.2)$$

and the optimal punitive award would be:

$$X_i^* = \frac{1-p_i\ell}{p_i\ell}H \qquad (3.4.3)$$

for all i, where p_i is the probability of detection associated with victim i.[7] Thus, a different punitive award for the same harm is not an indication of inefficiency. In fact, it could be an improvement in efficiency, under certain conditions—as detailed in Section 3.6.

However, if we impose the (equity) condition that:

$$D_1 = D_2 = ... = D_n,$$ (3.4.4)

then there is a unique D^* that solves the equation $\sum E(D_i^*) = nH$, which achieves optimal deterrence:

$$D_i^* = \frac{\theta n H}{\ell[(1-(1-\theta)^n)p_1 + (\theta n - 1 + (1-\theta)^n)p_2]}$$ (3.4.5)

or

$$D_i^* = \frac{p_1 z(nH)}{(1-(1-\theta)^n)p_1 + (\theta n - 1 + (1-\theta)^n)p_2}.$$ (3.4.5')

for all i. The punitive portion of D_i^* can be expressed as:

$$X_i^* = \left(\frac{p_1 z n}{(1-(1-\theta)^n)p_1 + (\theta n - 1 + (1-\theta)^n)p_2} - 1 \right) H,$$ (3.4.6)

where $\dfrac{p_1 z n}{(1-(1-\theta)^n)p_1 + (\theta n - 1 + (1-\theta)^n)p_2} - 1$ is the punitive multiplier.

Again, the formulas are based on the assumption that all the victims receive a uniform damage payment. The influence of publicity is evident by the fact that the formulas are a mixture of both p_1 and p_2. Additionally, the calculations are dependent on the number of victims, which is not the case for the traditional formula. Otherwise,

---

[7] Under the present assumption, p_i is either p_1 or p_2.

(3.4.5) and (3.4.6) are not particularly intuitive and are best understood by examining the relationship between the parameters and the size of X_i^*, which is presented in the following section.

3.5   Comparing the Results

For a comparison, equations (3.4.6) and (3.3.7) will be referred to as the optimal punitive damage payment under the dynamic, X_D^*, and static, X_S^*, approaches, respectively.

Proposition 1. *For all $n > 1$ and non-zero values for the remaining parameters,*

$$X_D^* < X_S^*.$$

Essentially, the static multiplier is a special case of the dynamic multiplier when there is no chance of publicity after a verdict, i.e., $z = 0$, since

$$\lim_{z \to 0} X_D^* = \frac{H}{p_1 \ell}. \tag{3.5.1}$$

As an illustration of the difference between X_D^* and X_S^*, assume $n = 10$, $p_1 = 0.1$, $p_2 = 0.4$, $\ell = 0.5$, and $z = 0.5$. If $H = \$1,000$, then $X_S^* = \$19,000$ with a punitive multiplier of 19, while $X_D^* = \$14,198$ with a punitive multiplier of 14.2, which is the optimal level, given the change in the probability of detection.

Thus, when there is a positive possibility of publicity, the use of the static multiplier results in excess deterrence. Of greater interest is the influence that the key parameters of the model (z, p_2, and n) have on the magnitude of the deterrence error.

Proposition 2. *The value of $X_S^* - X_D^*$ increases the more likely a successful verdict will be publicized (i.e., as z approaches 1).*

For example, automotive and medical product liability cases are more likely to be widely publicized than cases involving fraud from an insurance contract. If so, then a judge or jury setting the punitive award should adjust the award depending on whether the probability of publicity is high or low. In addition to the likelihood of publicity, the strength of the publicity should also be considered in setting the award.

Proposition 3. *The value of $X_S^* - X_D^*$ increases the greater influence the publicity has on changing the uncompensated victims' probability of detection (i.e., as p_2 approaches 1).*

If the revised probability of detection, p_2, does equal 1, then the triggered publicity causes all the remaining victims to detect the harm. In this case, there are no uncompensated victims; therefore, the optimal punitive damage payment, X_D^*, will fall. The extent of the decrease will depend on the original probability of detection, p_1. Given this result, it follows that the gap between the static and dynamic approach, $X_S^* - X_D^*$, gets larger as p_2 approaches 1.

Proposition 4. *The value of $X_S^* - X_D^*$ increases as the total number of victims increase (i.e., as n gets larger).*

Since a possible revision in detection does not influence the value of the static multiplier, the number of victims has no influence. However, with publicity, the injurer expects to pay more in total *compensatory* damages; therefore, the punitive award should be reduced to reflect this change. Additionally, with more victims, there are more successful verdicts to possibly trigger the publicity. Thus, as n approaches ∞, for a given level of z, the more influence p_2 has on the multiplier relative to p_1.

Using simulations, Appendix B compares the two multipliers. There are four tables where the row and column variables are p_1 and p_2, respectively, ranging in value from 10% to 90%. The tables differ in the parameter values for the probability of publicity (z) and the number of victims (n). The static multipliers are in bold and occur when $p_1 = p_2$, since

$$\lim_{p_2 \to p_1} X^*_D = X^*_S.$$ (3.5.2)

The simulations highlight the major differences between the two multipliers. The static multipliers are independent of the probability of publicity and the number of victims, thus they are the same across the four tables. The dynamic multipliers are the closest to the static ones in the first table where z is 25% and there are 10 victims. As an illustration of Propositions 2 and 4, the most dramatic difference between the two approaches is in the last table where z increases to 50% and there are 100 victims. If the initial probability of detection is 10% ($p_1 = 0.1$), then the static multiplier is 9. However, after publicity, if the probability of detection increases to 90% ($p_2 = 0.9$), then the dynamic multiplier is 0.349. For a $100,000 harm, this translates into a $865,100 difference between the two punitive awards.

3.6   Litigation Costs

In the previous section, uniform and heterogeneous damage awards are equivalent in terms of efficiency. However, if we introduce positive litigation costs for the victims,

14

then the choice between uniform and heterogeneous awards could impact efficiency. The idea is that, with a uniform award, the first victim might not have enough incentive to sue. If the victim does not sue, then there is no possibility of publicity and further litigation. The result is no deterrence and too much harm. Conversely, with heterogeneous awards, under certain litigation cost conditions, the first victim has an incentive to sue and trigger publicity which results in efficiency.

Formally, a victim makes the decision to sue as long as the expected benefit, $E(B)$, is greater than the expected cost, $E(C)$. Assume that the victim's total opportunity cost of litigation is c. Thus, the expected cost of litigation is simply:

$$E(C) = c. \tag{3.6.1}$$

Additionally, assume that the victim's cost is not a function of the injurer's litigation cost.

The victim's expected benefit from litigation depends on (i) whether the harm is discovered without the aid of publicity (i.e., the "first cohort," who have a p_1 probability of detection)[8] or with publicity (i.e., the "second cohort," who have a p_2 probability of detection) and (ii) whether the courts award uniform or heterogeneous awards. Assuming risk-neutrality, regardless of the type of award, the expected benefit to the first cohort is

$$E(B_1) = p_1 \ell D^*. \tag{3.6.2}$$

The expected benefit to the second cohort is

$$E(B_2) = p_2 \ell D^*. \tag{3.6.3}$$

---

[8] In the context of this section, all victims know they are harmed and "detection" occurs when they find out who is responsible. More realistically, p incorporates the probability of liability, although the analysis will keep them separate for consistency.

If courts award uniform damage payments, then $D^* = D_U^*$, which is equal to the optimal uniform award derived in Section 3.4. For heterogeneous awards, the optimal award depends on whether you are in the first or second cohort. If you are in the first cohort, then $D^* = D_1^* = \dfrac{H}{p_1 \ell}$. If you are in the second cohort, then $D^* = D_2^* = \dfrac{H}{p_2 \ell}$.

Given that $p_1 < p_2$, it follows that $D_1^* > D_2^*$. In comparison, since the uniform damage award uses a combination of p_1 and p_2, D_U^* falls between the two possible heterogeneous awards:

$$D_1^* > D_U^* > D_2^*. \tag{3.6.4}$$

The following table computes the expected benefit for each cohort under both uniform and heterogeneous awards.

Table 1: *Expected Benefit from Litigation*

	Uniform Award	Heterogeneous Award
First Cohort (i.e., $p_i = p_1$)	$[\, E(B_1)_U = p_1 \ell D_U^* \,] < H$	$[\, E(B_1)_\Sigma = p_1 \ell D_1^* \,] = H$
Second Cohort (i.e., $p_i = p_2$)	$[\, E(B_2)_U = p_2 \ell D_U^* \,] > H$	$[\, E(B_2)_\Sigma = p_2 \ell D_2^* \,] = H$

Relationship Summary: $E(B_2)_U > [\, E(B_1)_\Sigma = H = E(B_2)_\Sigma \,] > E(B_1)_U$.

The subscripts U and Σ denote uniform and non-uniform awards, respectively. One way to perceive why the expected benefit to the first cohort under the uniform award, $E(B_1)_U$, is less than the harm, H, is to note the expected benefit under the heterogeneous award, $E(B_1)_\Sigma$, is equal to the harm. The only difference between the two awards is that the optimal damage award, D^*, is higher under the heterogeneous award. The reverse logic holds for why the expected benefit to the second cohort under the uniform award, $E(B_2)_U$, is greater than the harm.

The table illustrates that the awards are not equivalent in terms of equity. The victims who discover the harm without the aid of publicity (i.e., the first cohort), prefer the heterogeneous award, D_1^*, over the uniform award, D_U^*, since $E(B_1)_\Sigma > E(B_1)_U$. However, the victims who discover the harm after publicity (i.e., the second cohort), prefer D_U^* over D_2^*, since $E(B_2)_U > E(B_2)_\Sigma$. Intuitively, under uniform awards, the second cohort is benefiting from the first cohort's difficulty in discovering the harm. This does not occur under heterogeneous awards since the second cohort's award is independent of the first cohort's award.

Again, with positive litigation costs, a victim will sue the injurer as long as the expected benefit, $E(B)$, is greater than the litigation cost, c. The following table illustrates four possible cost conditions (i.e., how c relates to Table 1's *Relationship Summary*) and whether or not uniform or heterogeneous awards achieve efficiency, given the condition.

Table 2: *Various Cost Conditions and the Efficiency Implication*

Cost Condition	Uniform Award	Heterogeneous Award
[1] $E(B_2)_U > [E(B_1)_\Sigma = H = E(B_2)_\Sigma] > E(B_1)_U > c$	*Efficient*	*Efficient*
[2] $E(B_2)_U > [E(B_1)_\Sigma = H = E(B_2)_\Sigma] > c > E(B_1)_U$	Inefficient	*Efficient*
[3] $E(B_2)_U > c > [E(B_1)_\Sigma = H = E(B_2)_\Sigma] > E(B_1)_U$	Inefficient	Inefficient
[4] $c > E(B_2)_U > [E(B_1)_\Sigma = H = E(B_2)_\Sigma] > E(B_1)_U$	Inefficient	Inefficient

Under cost condition [1], both uniform and heterogeneous awards are efficient since both the first and second cohorts have an incentive to sue under each award type. However, for cost condition [2], the litigation cost is now greater than the expected benefit to the first cohort under uniform awards, $E(B_1)_U$. Thus, there is no incentive for this group to sue, even though the cost of litigation is less than the harm, H. This fact reflects the uncertain nature of discovering who the responsible party is and legally proving it even though a victim knows he has been harmed. Conversely, for cost condition [2], a heterogeneous award is efficient because the expected benefit to the first cohort, $E(B_1)_\Sigma$, is greater than the litigation cost. The same holds for the second cohort. This leads to the following proposition.

Proposition 5. *Under certain litigation cost conditions, moving from a uniform punitive award to heterogeneous awards is efficient.*

Under cost conditions [3] and [4], the first cohort has no incentive to sue under either uniform or heterogeneous awards. Since the first cohort has no incentive to sue, there is no possibility of publicity and a formation of the second cohort. Nonetheless, efficiency can still be achieved if we use another form of heterogeneous awards. Courts could award damage payments to only the first victim who sues. In this case, the optimal damage award would be

$$E(B_1) = p_1 \ell D^* = nH,\qquad(3.6.5)$$

which reflects the idea that the first victim is compensated for the entire social harm, nH. The optimal damage payment that solves for the above equality is

$$D^* = \frac{nH}{p_1 \ell}.\qquad(3.6.6)$$

This would maximize the incentive to sue and minimize the total social litigation cost. One problem with this approach is that there will be a race to be the first one to initiate a suit.[9] The courts could mitigate this race to be first if they allow a waiting period before

---

[9] Additionally, there could be a race to be the first victim. The reason for this possible moral hazard is that the first victim's expected damages, from (3.6.6), is nH, which is greater than the original harm, H.

18

damages are paid in order to process all claims that are filed. Subsequently, they could treat each victim that filed equally in terms of damage payments.

As an example, suppose a producer can develop a piece of software with no bugs or with some bugs, which harms 100 users ($n = 100$) at $1,000/each ($H = \$1,000$) for a total harm of $100,000. If it only costs the manufacturer $10,000 to debug the product, then it should debug the software for a net social gain of $90,000. Initially, assume that the users suspect some bugs in the program, but there is only a 25% ($p_1 = 0.25$) chance they can find and document the bugs. Once the bugs are found, assume that the probability of liability is 100% ($\ell = 1$). Suppose that there is a 50% chance that a successful verdict will result in publicity ($z = 0.5$), which will increase the probability of detection to 75% ($p_2 = 0.75$). According to these set of facts: $D_1^* = \$4,000$, $D_U^* = \$1,408.45$, and $D_2^* = \$1,333.33$. Suppose the first victim's litigation cost is $500 ($c = \$500$). If the victim expects to be awarded the uniform award of $1,408.45, then there is no incentive to hire a lawyer and sue since the expected benefit is only $352.11 (0.25 times $1,408.45). If the injurer is aware of this lack of incentive to sue, then the debugging will not occur, and there is a net social loss of $90,000. However, if the first victim is awarded the heterogeneous award of $4,000, then the expected benefit, which is $1,000 (0.25 times $4,000), is greater than the litigation cost of $500. Thus, there is an incentive to sue, and the injurer will exercise the optimal amount of care and debug the product. In this example, a move to the heterogeneous award achieves efficiency as long as $\$1,000 > c > \$352.11$. If the cost is below $352.11, then both uniform and heterogeneous awards achieve efficiency. If the cost is above $1,000, then neither approach achieves efficiency.

Although, in this last situation, from equation (3.6.6), if we only give a damage

payment to the first victim equal to $400,000 ($100,000 divided by 0.25), which implies

an expected benefit of $100,000, then we achieve optimal deterrence and minimize the

social cost of litigation, as long as the litigation cost is less than $100,000.

In sum, the introduction of litigation costs can make the choice between uniform

and heterogeneous awards more than just one of equity. Under certain circumstances, it

can have an impact on efficiency.

4   Policy Implications

The main results of the previous section are (i) publicity matters and (ii)

heterogeneous punitive awards can be more efficient than uniform awards. One area

where these results are particularly applicable is when appellate courts review lower

courts' punitive damages awards. From the framework developed in the model, a

reduction in the initial punitive award is justifiable if (a) there is a probability that the

damage payment will create information for uncompensated victims *and* (b) the lower

court or jury did not account for (a).

For example, in *BMW of North America, Inc. v. Gore*[10] the appeals courts reduced

the initial punitive award. In that case, Ira Gore sought damages from BMW for selling

him a "new" car after it was repainted. Using the additional fact that, since 1983, BMW

had repainted 983 cars at a lost market value of $4,000/each ($H = \$4,000$), the trial court

awarded Ira Gore $4,000 in compensatory damages and $4 million in punitive damages

(technically, the punitive award should have been $4,000/car x 983 cars = $3.932

---

[10] 517 U.S. 559, 134 L. Ed. 809, 116 S. Ct. 1589 (1996).

million).[11] Within the framework of the static approach, the court indirectly assumed that 1 in 984 ($p_1 = 0.001$) would be successful in collecting their lost value of $4,000. This could turn out to be correct, but, as noted in Rubin, Calfee, and Grady (1997, p. 198), there is also a strong possibility that this case will lead to further litigation for BMW. Subsequently, the appeals court adjusted the punitive award to $2 million. On further appeal, the Supreme Court ruled that even a $2 million award was excessive, given the circumstances. Finally, the punitive award was remanded and subsequently reduced to $50,000 by the Supreme Court of Alabama.[12] Thus, if we include the compensatory damages, Ira Gore was ultimately awarded $54,000 ($D_U^* = \$54,000$).

Under the framework of the dynamic model, we can use information from the case to reasonably infer the implicit value for p_2 (i.e., the probability of detection after publicity) that the courts used to adjust the award. Given $n = 984$, the courts established 1/984 would be successful in court, which corresponds with a $p_1 = 0.001$ and $\ell = 1$.[13] If we assume that publicity is certain (i.e., $z = 1$), then the Supreme Court of Alabama was implicitly assuming a new probability of detection of approximately 196/984 (i.e.,

$p_2 = 0.2$).

However, in reality, it is unlikely that the various courts' actions in *BMW* can be accurately fitted into the framework established in this paper. The above revised probability of detection could very well be the courts' view of the original probability of

---

[11] This discussion assumes that, in *BMW v. Gore*, some positive level of punitive damages is appropriate. If we assume that the harm was non-intentional and BMW's behavior was efficient *ex ante*, then punitive damages does not improve efficiency. See Rubin, Calfee, and Grady (1997) for further discussion.
[12] 701 So. 2d 507 (1997); 1997 Ala. LEXIS 126.
[13] Or another combination where their product is 0.001. However, each combination will result in a unique p_2.

detection. Additionally, the courts might have had differing views on whether other victims should be able to collect punitive damages and, if so, how much.[14] This, in turn, would influence their decision on the amount of punitive damages.

Finally, can courts be expected to practically estimate the likelihood of publicity, z, the extent of the publicity, p_2, and the number of victims, n, which are three key parameters needed to properly determine punitive awards? Although there is no flawless approach, there are several ways in which a court could reasonably estimate the influence of publicity on the other victims. As previously noted, the information burden on the appellate courts will likely be lower, given that they can actually observe whether the case has caused publicity and whether other victims have filed claims. Thus, they can adjust the punitive amount appropriately.[15] Clearly, the facts of a particular case will also assist in a determination of the likelihood and strength of the publicity: the injuring firm's industry (automotive and pharmaceutical cases are likely to be highly publicized), the nature of the harm (health related cases are more likely to be publicized than purely financial ones), the demographic profile of the victims (all else equal, the elderly are more likely targets of fraud and less likely to be exposed to publicity), the spread of the harm (the strength of the publicity from local cases is likely to be great due to word-of-mouth), and the injuring firm's subsequent actions (if the firm issues a recall or a new warning label, then publicity is more likely).

---

[14] See Andrea G. Nadel's summary in 11 A.L.R.4th 1261 of the various legal opinions on the issue of awarding multiple punitive damages for the same harm. Generally, there is no legal principle that prohibits multiple awards.

[15] If the appeals courts systematically consider publicity when adjusting punitive awards, it is conceivable that a firm might try to encourage other victims to sue in order to "increase the publicity" and decrease the punitive award. Subsequently, the firm will try to settle with these other victims at some amount less than the decreased punitive award. However, this strategy is subject to a great deal of uncertainty given the potential for opportunistic behavior on the part of the victims, the potential for even more publicity, and the transaction costs of actually finding and negotiating with the other victims.

5 Conclusion

Whether or not courts choose uniform or different punitive awards, the publicity of successful verdicts changes people's behavior. The result is that, for uniform awards, the optimal punitive award—as compared to the standard result—is lower the more likely publicity will occur, the stronger the effect of the publicity, and the greater the number of victims. Additionally, both uniform and different punitive awards can achieve efficiency. The choice between the two depends on the extent of the victim's litigation cost. If the cost is substantial, then, under certain conditions, a clearly announced transition from uniform to heterogeneous punitive awards improves efficiency.

Proof of Proposition 1.

The difference between the two punitive awards is

$$X_S^* - X_D^* = \left(\frac{1}{\ell p_1} - \frac{p_1 z n}{(1-(1-\theta)^n)p_1 + (\theta n - 1 + (1-\theta)^n)p_2} \right) H . \tag{P1.1}$$

If $0 < p_1, p_2, z < 1$; $0 < \ell \leq 1$; $H > 0$; and $n > 1$; then $X_S^* - X_D^* > 0$ if and only if:

$$\frac{1}{\ell p_1} > \frac{p_1 z n}{(1-(1-\theta)^n)p_1 + (\theta n - 1 + (1-\theta)^n)p_2} \tag{P1.2}$$

or

$$(1-(1-\theta)^n)p_1 + (\theta n - 1 + (1-\theta)^n)p_2 > \theta n p_1 . \tag{P1.3}$$

Equation (P1.3) reduces to the following expression:

$$(\theta n - 1 + (1-\theta)^n)p_2 - (\theta n - 1 + (1-\theta)^n)p_1 > 0 \tag{P1.4}$$

which further reduces to:

$$p_2 > p_1 , \tag{P1.5}$$

which holds given the assumption from Section 3.1. Therefore, $X_S^* - X_D^* > 0$. **Q.E.D.**

Proof of Proposition 2.

The derivative of the difference of the two punitive awards, $(X_S^* - X_D^*)$, with respect to the probability of publicity, z, must be positive:

$$\frac{\partial(X_S^* - X_D^*)}{\partial z} > 0 . \tag{P2.1}$$

If $0 < p_1, p_2 < 1$; $0 < \ell \leq 1$; $H > 0$ (for simplicity, H is assumed to be 1, which makes (P2.1) the derivative of the punitive multipliers); and $n > 1$; then the derivative is equal to:

$$\frac{\theta n^2 p_1 p_2}{\left((1-(1-\theta)^n)p_1 + (\theta n - 1 + (1-\theta)^n)p_2 \right)^2}$$
$$- \frac{n p_1}{(1-(1-\theta)^n)p_1 + (\theta n - 1 + (1-\theta)^n)p_2} . \tag{P2.2}$$

If (P2.2) is positive, then the following holds:

$$\frac{\theta n p_2}{(1-(1-\theta)^n)p_1 + (\theta n - 1 + (1-\theta)^n)p_2} > 1 \tag{P2.3}$$

or

$$\theta n p_2 - (1-(1-\theta)^n)p_1 - (\theta n - 1 + (1-\theta)^n)p_2 > 0 . \tag{P2.4}$$

Equation (P2.4) reduces to:

$$0 > (-1 + (1-\theta)^n)(p_2 - p_1) \tag{P2.5}$$

or

$$1 > (1-\theta)^n.$$ (P2.6)

Since $\theta = p_1 \ell z$, θ is a positive number less than one, which implies that $(1-\theta)^n$ is less than one for all $n > 1$. **Q.E.D.**

Proof of Proposition 3.

The derivative of the difference of the two punitive awards, $(X_S^* - X_D^*)$, with respect to the revised probability of detection, p_2, must be positive:

$$\frac{\partial(X_S^* - X_D^*)}{\partial p_2} > 0.$$ (P3.1)

If $0 < p_1, z < 1$; $0 < \ell \leq 1$; $H > 0$ (H is assumed to be 1); and $n > 1$; then the derivative is equal to:

$$\frac{np_1 z(\theta n - 1 + (1-\theta)^n)}{\left((1-(1-\theta)^n)p_1 + (\theta n - 1 + (1-\theta)^n)p_2\right)^2}.$$ (P3.2)

If (P3.2) is positive, then the following is true:

$$np_1 z(\theta n - 1 + (1-\theta)^n) > 0,$$ (P3.3)

which reduces to:

$$(-1 + (1-\theta)^n) + \theta n > 0.$$ (P3.4)

From Proposition 2's equation (P2.6), we know $(-1 + (1-\theta)^n)$ is positive. Therefore, since θn is also positive, equation (P3.4) holds. **Q.E.D.**

Proof of Proposition 4.

The derivative of the difference of the two punitive awards, $(X_S^* - X_D^*)$, with respect to the total number of victims, n, must be positive:

$$\frac{\partial(X_S^* - X_D^*)}{\partial n} > 0.$$ (P4.1)

If $0 < p_1, p_2, z < 1$; $0 < \ell \leq 1$; $H > 0$ (H is assumed to be 1); and $n > 1$; then the derivative is equal to:

$$\frac{p_1 zn((-(1-\theta)^n \log(1-\theta))p_1 + (\theta + (1-\theta)^n \log(1-\theta))p_2)}{\left((1-(1-\theta)^n)p_1 + (\theta n - 1 + (1-\theta)^n)p_2\right)^2}$$
$$- \frac{p_1 z}{(1-(1-\theta)^n)p_1 + (\theta n - 1 + (1-\theta)^n)p_2},$$ (P4.2)

which reduces to:

$$n((-(1-\theta)^n \log(1-\theta))p_1 + (\theta + (1-\theta)^n \log(1-\theta))p_2) > .$$
$$(1-(1-\theta)^n)p_1 + (\theta n - 1 + (1-\theta)^n)p_2.$$ (P4.3)

Equation (P4.3) can be further reduced to:

$$1-(1-\theta)^{n}+n(1-\theta)^{n}\,log(1-\theta)>0. \tag{P4.4}$$

The derivative of the expression on the left-hand side of (P4.4) with respect to θ is

$$-n^{2}(1-\theta)^{n-1}\,log(1-\theta), \tag{P4.5}$$

which is positive given that $0<\theta<1$ and, thus, $log(1-\theta)<0$. Therefore, the expression is strictly increasing in θ. So if we evaluate the expression at $\theta=0$, which is the lowest limit value for θ, we get 0. Therefore, if $\theta>0$, equation (P4.4) holds.

Q.E.D.

Appendix B

Simulations

$z = 0.25$, $n = 10$, $\ell = 1$

$p_1 \backslash p_2$	0.1	0.2	0.3	0.4	0.5	0.6	0.7	0.8	0.9
0.1	*9*	8.047	7.260	6.599	6.035	5.550	5.127	4.756	4.427
0.2		*4*	3.550	3.175	2.857	2.584	2.347	2.139	1.956
0.3			*2.333*	2.050	1.811	1.608	1.431	1.277	1.141
0.4				*1.5*	1.299	1.128	0.981	0.853	0.741
0.5					*1*	0.848	0.717	0.604	0.505
0.6						*0.666*	0.546	0.443	0.352
0.7							*0.428*	0.331	0.246
0.8								*0.25*	0.169
0.9									*0.111*

$z = 0.5$, $n = 10$, $\ell = 1$

$p_1 \backslash p_2$	0.1	0.2	0.3	0.4	0.5	0.6	0.7	0.8	0.9
0.1	*9*	7.350	6.168	5.279	4.586	4.031	3.576	3.197	2.876
0.2		*4*	3.257	2.707	2.282	1.945	1.671	1.443	1.251
0.3			*2.333*	1.886	1.545	1.275	1.058	0.878	0.727
0.4				*1.5*	1.196	0.957	0.766	0.609	0.477
0.5					*1*	0.778	0.601	0.456	0.335
0.6						*0.666*	0.497	0.360	0.245
0.7							*0.428*	0.295	0.185
0.8								*0.25*	0.142
0.9									*0.111*

$z = 0.25$, $n = 100$, $\ell = 1$

$p_1 \backslash p_2$	0.1	0.2	0.3	0.4	0.5	0.6	0.7	0.8	0.9
0.1	*9*	5.128	3.417	2.453	1.835	1.404	1.087	0.844	0.651
0.2		*4*	2.569	1.775	1.270	0.921	0.665	0.469	0.314
0.3			*2.333*	1.586	1.112	0.785	0.546	0.363	0.219
0.4				*1.5*	1.040	0.724	0.492	0.315	0.176
0.5					*1*	0.689	0.461	0.288	0.152
0.6						*0.666*	0.442	0.271	0.136
0.7							*0.428*	0.258	0.125
0.8								*0.25*	0.117
0.9									*0.111*

$z = 0.5$, $n = 100$, $\ell = 1$

$p_1 \backslash p_2$	0.1	0.2	0.3	0.4	0.5	0.6	0.7	0.8	0.9
0.1	*9*	4.551	2.842	1.938	1.378	0.997	0.722	0.513	0.349
0.2		*4*	2.448	1.631	1.127	0.785	0.538	0.351	0.204
0.3			*2.333*	1.542	1.054	0.724	0.485	0.304	0.162
0.4				*1.5*	1.020	0.694	0.459	0.282	0.142
0.5					*1*	0.677	0.445	0.269	0.131
0.6						*0.666*	0.435	0.260	0.123
0.7							*0.428*	0.254	0.118
0.8								*0.25*	0.114
0.9									*0.111*

References

Becker, Gary S., "Crime and Punishment: An Economic Approach," *Journal of Political Economy 76* (1968), pp. 169-217.

Cooter, Robert D., "Economic Analysis of Punitive Damages," *Southern California Law Review* 56 (1982), pp. 79-101.

Cooter, Robert D., "Punitive Damages for Deterrence: When and How Much?" *Alabama Law Review* 40 (1989), pp. 1143-96.

Cooter, Robert and Thomas Ulen, *Law and Economics*, 3rd edition, (Addison Wesley Longman, Inc., 2000).

Craswell, Richard, "Damage Multipliers in Market Relationships," *Journal of Legal Studies* 25 (1996), pp. 463-92.

Garber, Steven and Anthony G. Bower, "Newspaper Coverage of Automotive Product Liability Verdicts," *Law & Society Review* 33 (1999), pp. 93-122.

Landes, William M. and Richard A. Posner, *The Economic Structure of Tort Law* (Harvard University Press, 1987).

Polinsky, A. Mitchell and Steven S. Shavell, "Punitive Damages: An Economic Analysis," *Harvard Law Review* 111 (1998), pp. 870-962.

Rubin, Paul H., John E. Calfee, and Mark F. Grady, "*BMW v. Gore*: Mitigating the Punitive Economics of Punitive Damages," *Supreme Court Economic Review* 5 (1997), pp. 179-216.

Shavell, Steven, *Economic Analysis of Accident Law*, (Harvard University Press, 1987).

U.S. Department of Justice, *Health Care Fraud Report, Fiscal Year 1997* (1997).

Viscusi, W. Kip, "The Social Costs of Punitive Damages Against Corporations in Environmental and Safety Torts," *Georgetown Law Review* 87 (1998), pp. 285-345.

www.ingramcontent.com/pod-product-compliance
Lightning Source LLC
Chambersburg PA
CBHW081247170526
45165CB00009B/3234